KING CRAB IS COMING!

Written by Damian Harvey
Illustrated by Sholto Walker

Harcourt
Supplemental Publishers

Rigby • Steck-Vaughn

www.steck-vaughn.com

Contents

In the Rock Pool

King Crab lived all alone in a small pool by the sea. On some days, the tide brought fish to his pool. The fish told King Crab about the deep blue sea.

But when the tide went out, the fish went away. King Crab was alone again. "I'm tired of being alone in this pool," King Crab said one day. "I will go out to sea and meet all the fish."

Little Shrimp was hiding under a rock. "Oh, no!" Little Shrimp said to himself. "King Crab is going out to sea and eat all the fish!"

When the tide came in, King Crab left his pool. He went out into the open sea.

King Crab went by Little Shrimp. Little Shrimp saw King Crab's claws. They were very big. Little Shrimp was scared.

"I must tell Small Fish that King Crab is coming," said Little Shrimp. "She is wise. She will know what to do." Little Shrimp swam off into the open sea to look for Small Fish.

Out to Sea

Small Fish was swimming around some tall reeds. Little Shrimp came along. "Small Fish! Small Fish!" cried Little Shrimp. "King Crab is coming!"

"Why should I care about King Crab?" asked Small Fish.

Just then, King Crab himself went by. He had sand in his eyes and his mouth. His claws clattered because the water was cold. "I don't like the deep blue sea," he said. "But I do want to meet all the fish."

Little Shrimp and Small Fish could hear King Crab's clattering claws.

"That's why you should care about King Crab!" cried Little Shrimp. "Because he has big clattering claws! He's going to **eat** all the fish!"

"We should go and see Big Squid," said Small Fish. "He is wise. He will know what to do."

Little Shrimp and Small Fish swam down into the ocean to look for Big Squid.

Going Deep

Big Squid was swimming by some rocks when Little Shrimp and Small Fish came along. "Big Squid! Big Squid!" cried Small Fish. "King Crab is coming!"

"Why should I care about King Crab?" asked Big Squid.

Just then, King Crab himself went by. The water had grown colder. His claws clattered, and his jaws chattered. "It is very cold down in the deep blue sea," said King Crab. "But I really want to **meet** all the fish."

Little Shrimp, Small Fish, and Big Squid could hear King Crab's clattering claws. They could hear his chattering jaws.

"That's why you should care about King Crab!" cried Small Fish. "Because he has big clattering claws and mean chattering jaws. He's going to eat all the fish!"

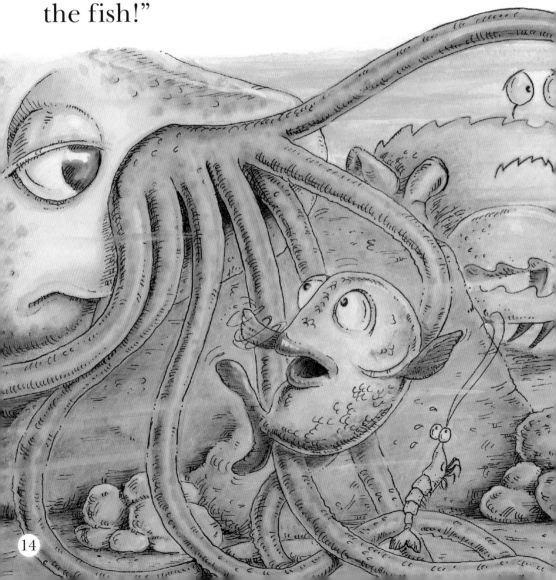

Big Squid said, "We must go deep into the ocean to see Giant Whale. She is wiser than anyone. She will know what to do."

Little Shrimp, Small Fish, and Big Squid swam off to look for Giant Whale deep down in the ocean.

Giant Whale was asleep when Little Shrimp, Small Fish, and Big Squid came along. "Giant Whale! Giant Whale!" cried Big Squid. "King Crab is coming!"

Giant Whale opened one eye. "Why should I care about King Crab?" she asked.

Just then, King Crab himself went by. He was very cold. His claws were clattering, and his jaws were chattering. "It is very cold down in the deep blue sea," he said. "But I really want to **meet** all the fish."

King Crab looked around. "Hello!" he called out. His hello came out like a roar.

Little Shrimp, Small Fish, Big Squid, and Giant Whale could hear King Crab's clattering claws and his chattering jaws. They could hear his roar.

"That's why you should care about King Crab!" shouted Big Squid to Gaint Whale. "Because he has big clattering claws and mean chattering jaws! He has the biggest roar in the ocean! He's going to eat all the fish in the sea!"

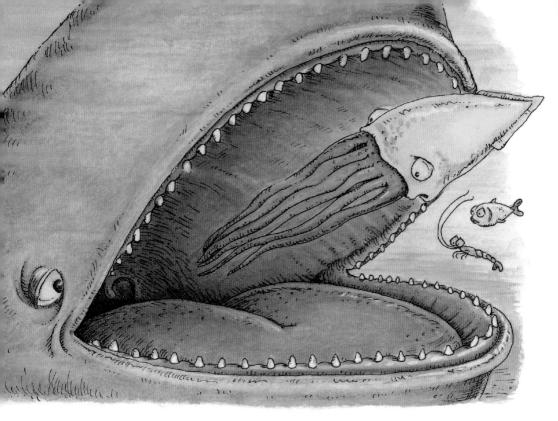

Little Shrimp, Small Fish, and Big Squid waited for Giant Whale to speak. Then Giant Whale said, "You must hide in my mouth until King Crab has gone."

Little Shrimp, Small Fish, and Big Squid looked at each other. Then the three of them swam into Giant Whale's open mouth.

Going Home

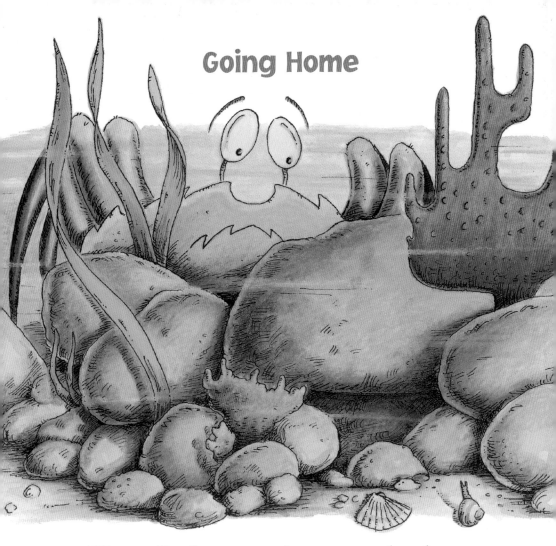

King Crab went down to the bottom of the sea. He couldn't see anyone. He looked behind rocks. Then he swam to the top of a hill. But he still couldn't see anyone.

The ocean was big and cold. King Crab was very tired. He wanted to be back in his small pool by the sea.

King Crab swam back to his pool.
He was very happy to be home and
not under the deep blue sea.

Deep down in the ocean, Giant Whale opened her mouth. Little Shrimp, Small Fish, and Big Squid swam out. Giant Whale smiled to herself and went back to sleep.